SEBITICALS

CHAPTER X

NANA AWERE DAMOAH

SEBITICALS

CHAPTER X

DAkpabli

Also by Nana Awere Damoah

MY BOOK OF #GHCOATS
QUOTES BY NAD
NSEMPIISMS
SEBITICALLY SPEAKING
I SPEAK OF GHANA
TALES FROM DIFFERENT TAILS
THROUGH THE GATES OF THOUGHT
EXCURSIONS IN MY MIND

THE AUTHOR

Nana Awere Damoah holds a Master's degree in Chemical Engineering from the University of Nottingham, a Bachelor's in Chemical Engineering from the Kwame Nkrumah University of Science and Technology (KNUST) and a Postgraduate Diploma in Operations and Supply Chain Management from the University of Liverpool. A British Council Chevening alumnus, Nana works as a publisher, bookseller and technical services consultant.

In 1997, Nana won first prize in the Step Magazine National Writing Competition. He is the author of seven books: *Quotes by NAD*, *Nsempiisms*, *Sebitically Speaking*, *I Speak of Ghana*, *Tales from Different Tails*, *Through the Gates of Thought*, and *Excursions in my Mind*; and curator/editor of My Book of #GHCoats. He has also contributed to two anthologies. He keeps personal blogs at https://nanaaweredamoah.wordpress.com.

In January 2017, Nana Damoah featured as 'Author of the Month' by KWEE, a Liberian Literary magazine. In the 60th Anniversary edition of the Ghana Association of Writers Awards held in November (also to mark Ghana@60), Nana won first prize in the Ama Ata Aidoo Story Writing Category with his story *October Rush* (published in his book *Tales from Different Tails*).

He is married with three children and is based in Tema.

Dedicated to the memory of my forebears, Nana Premang Ntow II and Kasapreko Nana Kwame Bassanyin III

SECOND SEBITICALS

II Sebiticals
Chapter 1

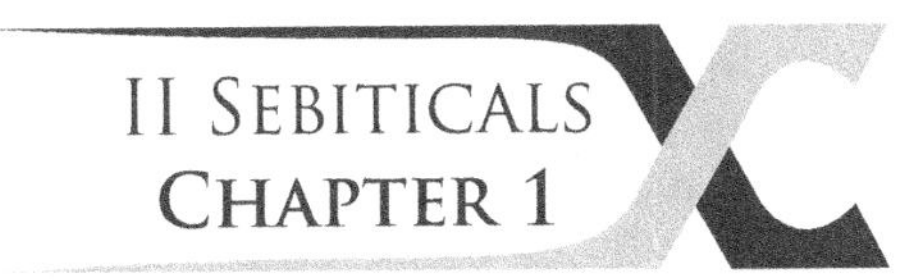

A Century On, A Man Born Not of Yaa Asantewaa

Today, I start my Sebiticals with a proverb the obroni, Amy Engel, told in her nkrataa[1] She said: "I'm not sure how we got to this place, where a girl's only value is in what kind of marriage she has, how capable she is of keeping a man happy."

On 1 July 2014, a group of those people who prefer wearing tapoli[2] around their necks and wearing siketi[3] instead of ntama decided to join a motley band of young folks who wanted to do a walk to the Ahenfie[4]. They said they had some words they wanted Odikro to hear. A good number of our beautiful and strong ladies joined the march. After the event, some of the leading newspapers sympathetic to the ruling

---

[1] Nkrataa: Book
[2] Tapoli: Dumb-bell shaped wooden tool used for grinding in an earthware bowl (apotoyiwa)
[3] Siketi: Adulteration of the word 'skirt'
[4] Ahenfie: Chief's palace

government decided to defame at least three of the ladies. One was mocked because she was not married.

Sikaman has been reeling under the effect of what has been known as dumsor[5]. Some say there is so little sor that we should call it dumkoraa[6]. Odikro has been promising as usual and giving assurances he is not sure about. In March 2014, he said the crisis was temporary and asked for patience. Just over a year later, on May 1, 2015, he again said the situation was only temporary, and will be surmounted in the "not too distant future". This has led not a few people to enquire from the catechist whether the meaning of temporary has changed since the cedi's fall on the world market. Wofa Kapokyikyi, who was on his way back from the Liberty Fan Club and was infused with the spirit with the accompanying fuse, interjected by saying that the word 'temporary' should be appreciated in the spirit of the word 'provisional', which lasted for eleven years.

A number of the big men and women whose films we watch at Sadisco Hotel have been speaking about this dumkoraa situation. John Dum said his mind. And Lydia Forsuwaa too. And then John Dum came back to clarify what he said earlier.

There have been various reactions, of course, as always happens in Sikaman. Don't we even speak back to Amakye

[5]Dumsor: Power outage/load-shedding
[6]Dumkoraa (Twi): Dum means 'put off the lights', koraa means completely or permanently

the town crier when he gives us a message from Odekuro[7], though we know he is only a messenger?

However, one of the responses that really got me tongue-tied was from a man who is said to do some walatu-walasa near the Ahenfie. He said because Forsuwaa had no man on whose wall she could lean her gun against, she had no right to wield a gun.

When I first heard this, I thought to myself that when a woman speaks and all you have to say in return is based on whether she is married or not, then my comments for you are best retained in my head.

But my Wofa Kapokyikyi said I was a fool if I didn't unload the many thoughts in my mind about this. He is right because those thoughts were giving me headaches. So, I will speak.

As I said earlier, this misogynistic posturing was exhibited clearly last July after the OccupyFlagStaff House protest by some publications in Ghana. I said once that the beautiful thing about patience and the bosom of time is that words used to put someone in his/her place today will be the same words that embarrass or implicate the speaker tomorrow. In the matter of the current misogynistic utterances, however, the time lap is microscopic. It is, in this case interestingly, embedded in the proverb that says when you point the index finger at a person, three fingers are pointing back at you.

[7]Odikro: Chief of a town
[8]Abrewa: Old woman; wise woman

By the definition and categorisation applied at unmarried, above-thirty, ladies, the speaker paints a lot of his own colleagues and comrades.

The beauty of words.

The blessedness of time.

This is a country where in the early 1900s, a woman took up her gun and led men into battle.

This is a country where the selection of our chiefs and kings cannot happen unless the queenmother decides.

This is a country where when there is a dilemma and a difficult knot to be untied, we go to see Abrewa[8].

A century later, there arises a man who is so close to the Ahenfie telling us that because of the rope between his legs, he has more sense than his mother who created and nurtured that rope.

This is how far we have come. We are where we are.

A few days after the May Day celebrations, I had a chat with Professor H Kwasi Prempeh, a man who inspires me greatly. We discussed my new book, *Sebitically Speaking*, and he indicated thus: "Reading Sebiticals has been both fun and inspiring. We've got work to do. A lot."

I sought his permission to share some of the responses I gave to him in the conversation. I wrote thus: "Indeed we have. More so, on the minds of our people. The level of mental appreciation is so low, and it is complicated by the unwillingness to get enlightened."

Then, he said: "Absolutely. And it's getting worse on so many levels. We seem to be dumbing down, from top to bottom. I am so happy I am on social media. It's the one place where I encounter a community of compatriots, a small yet critical mass, that gives me hope that a revival is possible."

I continued: "Yes, I set out to use social media to change one mind at a time too. But it is also where one sees the magnitude of the problem."

I added that as a nation, social media has given us the privilege to see the thinking process of some of our political leaders; thoughts written not by speechwriters. Some of what is written is frightening.

We do need a renewal of our minds and very urgently. This misogyny at the highest and lowest levels of our society reflects something deeper: our deficiency in having intellectual discussions devoid of insults and personality attacks.

In my book, *I Speak of Ghana*, page 111, I wrote: "People would resort to insults rather than keep focus on the argument; and they do so when they have lost the capacity to debate intellectually."

We are where we are.

I have a little girl, who I am training to be assertive, intelligent, inquisitive, questioning and strong. I wish for her to be respected for her views as a human being. This is why this posturing must be condemned in no uncertain terms.

Which is why Wofa Kapokyikyi was right that I spoke my thoughts.

Which is why we should continue to empower our women to speak and to express themselves. To be confident. Not to be defined by what a man says they are by a ring. Or lack of it. We must cure this. If it is due to ignorance, we must preach enlightenment and banish it.

For as Joanna Russ said, "Ignorance is not bad faith. But persistence in ignorance is."

Finally, those who persist in this ignominy must be told that this is Sikaman. We crossed that pre-historic line when Yaa Asantewaa marched.

Till I come your way again with another sebitical, I remain:

Sebitically yours,

Kapokyikyiwofaase

Of Giving, Tithing and Accountability

Many years ago, I read a quote which I have been looking for in the past few months but can't find. The writer of the quote stated that he hardly gave advice on relationships (marriage) and religion, because he didn't want any persons to blame him (the writer) for their woes in this life or in the next.

I have generally followed that advice. I hardly write about direct religious advice and I can count only about two articles of mine which are dedicated to marriage. And this is out of over a hundred full articles I have written over the more than a decade of active writing.

Last week, actually on my birthday, 3 June 2015, Accra experienced one of the worst flooding I have seen in my life. This coincided with one of the worst fire incidents the nation has ever known as well, at a fuel station near Nkrumah Circle. Initial reports indicate that fuel from the tanker leaked and was carried on the surface of the flood waters to a nearby fire source. Over 150 people have been reported killed from that incident. Many of the dead were sheltering away from the rains when the fire started. A dear friend of mine had left the same fuel station just five minutes before the blast. The total death toll from the combined fire and flooding incidents is currently over 200.

May the souls of the departed rest in peace.

And may we who remain behind ensure that, together, we create the environment and nation that prevents such catastrophes from happening.

As we mourn, I believe that our faith should find expression in our response to the needs of the afflicted and poor around us, and in our giving to assuage their pains. Our faith should speak through acts of charity. For instance, the least we can do as Christian churches is to donate all offerings this month to relief efforts. We should do even more. Dip into our vaults and give succor to the afflicted.

Do an act of kindness this month.

Which is why over the weekend after the flooding, I used my Facebook page to engage my readers and followers on the principle and act of tithing, giving and accountability in our churches and religious organisations.

I have always maintained an unorthodox approach to tithing and how I disburse my tithes.

I was taught about tithing in the Scripture Union. Which is an evangelistic organisation. I felt comfortable then to give my tithes to SU and still do. So, my foundational appreciation of this duty is to give for the furtherance of Christian outreach.

My understanding is that when money is brought into the house of God (read: christian evangelistic organisation), it is to be used for three purposes: maintaining the house, supporting the workers in the house and feeding the outside world for which the house and religion exists: the poor, the afflicted and the needy.

So, I continue to tithe, which means I set aside a tenth of my income. And I give to chrisitian organisations and also give out to support outreaches. Outreaches here include to the poor, afflicted and needy.

Which means even when I see a needy student who needs funds to finish school, that person falls within my scope. If I see a poor person in my society, that person falls within my scope. If there is a project to bring relief to a community, it falls within my scope. I don't believe that my money needs to go through the conduit of an organisation for it to be blessed enough to express christian charity and love to a recipient.

Note that I haven't mentioned 'church' so far. I see that as a subset of the total universe I have defined above (recall your mathematics and sets).

I find many of our churches forgetting that we exist to affect our world and not necessarily only by the noise we make through our loudspeakers.

This month use your funds directly to affect a poor, afflicted or needy person.

This proposal generated a lot of responses and varied views. In our discussion on tithes, a few people made a submission that I summarize as below:

"Giving of tithes is an instruction and must go to my church. My responsibility is to obey that. How the money is used is not something I should concern myself with. It is something only the pastor(s) is/are accountable to God for."

I was, and am, still shocked. If accountability does not and cannot start from the church, then I am not sure how we can hold anyone accountable in this land.

Perhaps I have been 'spoilt' by my training and association with Joyful Way and Ridge Church.

Right from the beginning of my time in JWI, I was shocked with the detailed and tough questions asked at Annual General Meetings (AGM). We used to joke that if your first meeting as a JWI member was at an AGM, you would wonder if it was a christian organization, with the Executives questioned on their stewardship and accounts.

Audited accounts are circulated to everyone and lines of expenditure and income outlined are scrutinised. The Executives would give account for each year of stewardship.

The group has a constitution which governs it, and which is followed, with regular reviews as and when. The Executive body reports to a Board.

Ridge Church has its board, has Annual General Meetings (AGM) and accounts given each week on preceding week's inflows.

Perhaps my expectations of accountability in our churches are utopian.

But, back to the point of giving this month to help those affected.

Let me leave you with some more questions:

What did you do last weekend to help someone affected by the floods?

When was the last time your church did an outreach or donation to the needy, poor and afflicted?

Does your church have a program to support such people? Even within the church?

Do an act of charity this month.

Think about various ways you can help. A group of people could set up a hot-lunch spot today to share food with the communities affected by the floods. They need clothing, mattresses, water. A few people have set up fundraising activities; find one and support. You can lend a helping hand whether you are in Ghana or not.

You can also join efforts to clean up your community.

Whatever you do, don't be on the fence.

We are one another's keeper, and the shoes could be on your feet the next time.

Till I come your way again with another sebitical, I remain:

Sebitically yours,

Kapokyikyiwofaase

DONKORANTUMI – THE CHALKY ROAD TO ROME

I love reflecting on some of the old joys of my growing up years and, recently, I have been curating photos of yesteryears, which I have titled *Do You Remember?* These pictures tell us, somehow, of a past Ghana that was more structured and better organised than what we have now, reminding me that, in many ways, our Sikaman past seems brighter than our future. An entire topic for discussing in a sebitical soon.

Earlier this year, I indulged in watching old movies set in Ghana. No one can miss movies by Kwaw Ansah in such an exercise. So, I watched *Love Brewed in an African Pot*, *Heritage Africa* and *Kukurantumi: Road to Accra*.

In *Heritage Africa*, the main character, who wanted to appear and act more British than the Queen, had changed his name, Kwesi Atta Bosomefi, to Quincy Arthur Bosomfield and had risen to become the District Commissioner of Accra in

His Majesty's Gold Coast. One aspect of the film stayed with me. His mother, played by the legendary Alexandria Duah, gave him a family heirloom which had been passed on from generation to generation, amongst the male heads of the family. It was believed to carry "the soul and pride" of the Abusua; his late uncle had been the previous custodian and now it was Kwesi Atta's turn to hold it in safe custody, to be his source of strength and pride, to be held in trust and passed on to the next generation. As soon as his mum left, Kwesi took this family treasure to his office and showed it to his British boss, who expressed his admiration of the artifact. Kwesi asked his boss to keep it as a gift from him.

A few days later, Kwesi visited his mum in the village and the old lady's first question to him was whether he was keeping the heirloom safe. When Kwesi told her he had given it out to his boss, the mum wailed loudly and exclaimed: "Ebei Kwesi Atta Bosomefi! Sukuu pii yi a ekɔe yi, ennsua nyansa kakra enfir mu a?" meaning "after all your long years of schooling, did you not learn or gather any wisdom?" The film editor translated the question as "What happened to all the classroom education?"

In my holy village of Wasa Akropong, where my Wofa Kapokyikyi runs things, we say that there is a difference between home sense and school sense. Indeed, Kapokyikyi would say that adwen nko, na nyansa nko (not all who have brains have wisdom). It also means that knowledge must be applied with wisdom. For instance, a wise man knows when to open his mouth and when to close it, when to talk and when to hold back; wisdom is the right application of knowledge. I read once that knowledge is not power; it is the right application of knowledge that is power. Otherwise, there wouldn't be so many powerless knowledgeable people in this world. I bring you greetings from Wofa Kapokyikyi.

Wisdom is evident in whatever language it is expressed in. I have heard some foolish stuff expressed eloquently in English and have lapped at sense spoken in Twi. So, I don't get this so-called elitism because someone cannot speak English. Some of the wisest in our history have not been in classrooms and only a visit to a palace or rural gathering would confirm that.

Two incidents over the past week have set me on this excursion in my sebitical mind: the chalk talk in Kukurantumi (ah, it reminded me of Kwaw Ansah's Kukurantumi: Road to Accra) by the wife of Kontihene and the inclusion of Madam Akua Donkor on Odikro's visit to the Roman citadel.

The chalk talk, and the subsequent apology, brought to mind a story Wofa Kapokyikyi told me.

One Sunday morning, Opia was both broke and hungry, but he decided to still go to church in his Sunday best. He donned his white shirt over his favourite trousers and passed by Auntie Esi's chop bar to fill his stomach before church. He bought fufu with palm nut soup but couldn't afford meat. Auntie Esi put two pieces of okro on top of the fufu to decorate it.

Sitting by him on the bench was Nimo, whose fufu was surrounded by a guard of chunks of bush meat, with an assortment of dead goat legs – his delicacy.

Opia couldn't help but steal occasional glances at the meat pond in front of Nimo.

As Nimo tried to cut through the tough goat leg, one stubborn tendon stretched like a catapult and released a stream of palm soup which landed on the front of Opia's white shirt.

"I am so so sorry," Nimo immediately said.

"Sorry sɛn? Me de ɛyi nam (you can't just say sorry. I will take some of your meat as apology)!" Opia retorted, reaching out to Nimo's asanka.

Can we get the Kukurantumi apology in chalk, please?

In analysing the event, I found, first of all, that Kontihene's wife was telemo-ing a matter which wasn't hers to carry. The headmistress indicated that if you wanted to speak to God, you spoke to the wind. I have never heard the wind respond on God's behalf. Secondly, Kontihene's wife is not from the Sikaman Education Service which has rightly taken up the case but haven't provided any chalk yet. Finally, clearly, whatever message was intended to be transmitted in response to the chalk request was lost in translation. Wisdom and knowledge didn't converge.

Wofa Kapokyikyi tells me that this chalk talk is causing some headaches in the surrounding villages. As the election year approaches, the chiefs are expecting the politicians to remember the road to their respective villages. They are in a dilemma about what to say or not. Traditionally, they would ask for more support for their roads, hospitals and agriculture. Especially when the politicians from the ruling party visit. How would the responses be this time around? Would they be asked to reach out instead to the citizens of their villages home and away to support them instead? Would they be told that whatever the government is doing for them is only undeserved favour, even though it is done with their own taxes, from their sweat? Would they be told "We won't give you roads today or tomorrow?" Wofa tells me that the headaches are not responding yet to the ako balm.

As an aside, it must be tough being a social media political apparatchik. An issue breaks and you defend your party's interest like Kapokyikyiwofaase defending waakye. Then the person you are defending admits she erred and then you have to quickly find another tune to sing.

Spare a thought for such friends. The hustle is real.

When the new Oga Kpatakpata in Amalaman was being enstooled, Odikro, who played a pivotal role in engaging all sides of the political divide in the run-up to the elections, attended. At the same event, one of the leading opposition leaders in Sikaman, Madam Akua Donkor, was also seen at the ceremony. At the time, there was no official confirmation from Okyeame that Madam Donkor went on Odikro's tiasi nam. This week, Odikro was in Rome and when pictures emerged of those at the various functions, Madam Donkor was seen, with her trademark smile.

Ah, you know that Sikamanians can talk. Immediately, there were choruses of "What is she doing there?", "Can she even speak English?", "Why is she always on government trips?"

On the other hand, as usual, were those who drink palmwine with the Ahenfie guards and workers who retorted that the complaints were coming from people who walk with their noses in the air and think that because one doesn't speak English, that person couldn't think.

So, for the records and with the permission of Wofa Kapokyikyi, let Kapokyikyiwofaase insist that wisdom is clear in whichever language one speaks. So that shouldn't be an issue. A person who spews nonsense in English will sound the same when the message is translated into Hausa.

Beyond that, however, the questions must still be asked. Why is Madam Donkor on these official trips? Is it because she is an opposition leader? Is it because she is a farmer? What role was she playing on the Italy trip? Was it to gain insights at first-hand how agriculture can be linked directly to industry? Where is her farm? How does she represent the nominal farmer in Ghana?

In Sikaman, I find that we have difficulties in delineating policy questions from political questions and because we tend to make the messenger and the message joint from both the transmission and reception ends, most messages are lost and made redundant.

As someone posted on my Facebook timeline, even chalk leaves a political mark. Let's learn to distil all the wisdom we can from whoever we hear, and not raise any dust on our road to Kukurantumi.

Till I come your way again with another sebitical, I remain:

Sebitically yours,

Kapokyikyiwofaase

Even Long Vac Sef,
They Go a, They Dey Come!

Growing up in Kotobabi, one of the worst tragedies that could befall anyone was to be caught red-handed, stealing. Especially at dawn. Most of us lived in compound houses which were unwalled, so when a cry for help went out in the silence of dawn, neighbours could rally in minutes. Those were the days under the revolution when vigilante groups were recognised. Many of these groups were members of the Committee for the Defence of the Revolution (CDR). When a thief was caught, it was customary for him to be beaten mercilessly and escorted towards the big Alajo Gutter, which was more of a river than a gutter. It was that big. It had a distinctive smell too; years after, I can still smell it in my nostrils.

At the gutter, fortunate thieves got rescued by the police, who had to risk their lives to save these thieves. The unfortunate thieves got their home addresses changed to aquatic burial grounds. The treatment before the coup de grace varied in their gruesome creativity. Once, one guy got an enema of coal tar before being dispatched into glory. Or hell, to be more precise.

So, Akwesi Burger, a well-known criminal near the Maxwell Hotel area, considered himself lucky when he was rescued and sent to court, before being sentenced to ten years imprisonment with hard labour. One of those who really beat him up was Egya Nsiah, a painter. Akwesi never forgot him.

Ten years came quickly, and Akwesi was released from prison. On his way home, he came across Egya Nsiah painting the sides of a four-storey building. He looked up the ladder the painter was on and called out, loudly:

"Egya, I greet you!"

"Yaaaa nua!" Egya responded.

"Do you remember some years ago, a thief was caught near Nkansah Djan, and you were involved in getting him to the police?"

"Oh yes! I remember it like yesterday! I really beat him up to my heart's desire! He should have even been killed; such people don't deserve to like!"

Calmly, Akwesi held on the ladder and called out, "Well, I am that thief, and I never forgot how you thrashed me. Please find somewhere to stand, because I am taking this ladder away!"

In the name of Wofa Kapokyikyi who has the memory of an elephant and who says he can forgive, but never will forget, the man who says it as it is, I greet you.

It was Wofa who said that even though the bird flies and lives on a tree, when it dies its body comes back to earth.

In Form One in the school Osagyefo first built, the closest relative to The Wailers was a tall, fearsome senior of ours called Vandyke. For sure, his favourite expression was "Legalise it!" He who is in tune with the spirit of psychedelic delights will understand this.

One of the competencies that every junior needed to hone was the ability to run down the stairs from the top floor of the houses and exit the common room at the ground floor, hiding under the windows in front of the house to run across to the Academic areas without being spotted by the sharp eyes of those seniors who didn't go out of their dormitories except when there was fun fair or *scattey*[9] in the dining hall.

One day, one small boy ran down the stairs in Kwesi Plange House and didn't turn back when Senior Vandyke bellowed

[9]Scattey: A chaotic scramble for food in the dining hall

his name. It was mid-terms and the boy wasn't going back to the dormitory for all the *sɔpi*[10] in the dining hall! He knew if he did, he would end up being sent on errands the entire weekend.

As he ran off, Senior Vandyke chuckled and muttered to him, "Make you go! No bi mid-terms? Long vacation sef, they go a, they dey come back!"

The blessedness of time. Ah, the bosom of time disbosoms a tonne.

So it is that when people get into higher positions, they forget that the higher you are, the heavier you fall. But, time flies and even eight years come to pass, eventually.

Soon, both words and actions come full cycle. And the loss of power declutters the mind and descales the eyes.

Watch your words and actions, for soon, words and actions past answer the present. In other cases, words and actions present soon answer and judge the past.

I once said that the beautiful thing about patience and the bosom of time is that words used to put someone in his or her place today will be the same words that will embarrass or implicate the speaker tomorrow. Especially in this fast-paced world, time lap appears most microscopic.

[10]Sɔpi: Leftover food

Power has just changed in Sikaman and realignments are in progress. As the engine of the train exchanges placed with the caboose, let the engine reflect and let the caboose-turned-engine learn that even long vac sef, they go a, they dey come.

Till I come your way again with another sebitical, I remain:

Sebitically yours,

Kapokyikyiwofaase

II Sebiticals
Chapter 5

Sikaman Biegyarithms

In the fourth year after the old Odekuro Asomdwehene Obenefo Yohani Atta Nikanika died, there arose three men from the land of Montie who came shouting in the wilderness: "Make way for the Son of Drahama, Odekuro Okasafo Yohani Mahani Nikaboka, he who has been anointed to rule in the affairs of the land with yentie-obianic vim!"

And all the men and women and animals of the air, sea and land asked, "From whence cometh these folks who speaketh forth with vitriolic fervour?"

When the cries of the people reached the ears of Odekuro, he nodded and said the people needed elevation to see the source of the fervour that had taken hold of the Men of Montie.

Then the Men of Montie did the ultimate biegya and took the judges of the Supreme Council of the Ahenfie Court to the laundry behind Obaapanyin Potisaa's house, washing them clean and hanging them out to dry. When these men were summoned to the Council and asked to go sleep for some time in the stool room to reflect on their utterances, Odekuro went to the room under the cover of darkness and opened the door, releasing them to go, with the admonishment, "Go and biegya no more on the Council, but *toaso* on all others".

As they stepped out of the stool room, Amakye the town crier followed them with his afekyirewaa, singing, *Yentie Obiaa.*

Imbued with such royal encouragement, the Men of Montie proceeded to biegya, with all buccal cavities at full blast.

But trust Wofa Kapokyikyi, the life patron of Liberty Fan Club, whose motto toasonically remains yɛ bu didi and whose bitters is fortified with the choicest roots of Sikaman, to get to the root of the matter. He told me that the source of the montienic fervour was political akpeteshie.

From my elementary chemistry as taught by Teacher Johnson, the fuse from political akpeteshie exhibits both diffusive and osmotic tendencies, flowing from an area of high concentration to that of low concentration and also permeating all spheres of the society.

[11] A popular expression in the Wasa dialect, which translates loosely as 'we are going to consume it, it is not for sale'

Soon, this fervour found its way to royal rooms and, in a weird chain reaction that managed to defy the Vander Waals theorem, this fervour reacted with the gbeshinic catalyst and found not a few royal victims.

Come and see *biegya paa* from high places.

And, so, it came to pass that the custodians of our tradition decided to indulge in binge drinking of this political apio. One chief, who speaks with a similar tongue as we do in Wasa, used *bɛn kɔdi bɛn tɔn*[11] to express his wish to become a serial caller just to show how Odekuro has so transformed Sikaman that his lineage should rule forever. And the people of the Dormah said, "Omanhene, kasa!" With such loud encomiums, this chief proceeded to say that if he lost that argument as a serial caller, Nananom should have a say about his stool. But Nana was sly, he spoke in sebi-pothetical terms.

Many more chiefs spoke for and against Odekuro. It was a free-for-all royal biegyanisation. Political akpeteshie flowed on the land, and across it, ubiquitous like the Pra and the Volta in its reach.

But the biegyaest of all was the Omanhene of Gbese who got overtaken by all the seven spirits of Gbeshie and proclaimed that ɛbaa yi shie if Naa Toshie's friend ever gets a stool! Come and see clapping! "Twaa! Twaa! Omanye aba!" the people cried.

It has been said that when Nii saw the word *biegya*, which means *open fire* in Twi, the Ga word for fire, which is *la*, kikied him and made him to *la lala* (sing a song).

Odekuro heard the song and was pleased.

So, it came to pass when it had all passed that Naa Toshie's friend took the real commanding lead and cruised to victory.

The constitution of Sikaman enjoins chiefs to desist from drinking political akpeteshie, but this year, they decided that the cup that was used to serve Takyi should deservedly be extended to Baah. Afterall, man resembles nothing. They decided that being called fathers of their states amounted to little if they couldn't sip small for the stomach's sake. They decided that the tradition of a chief not eating in public was antediluvian.

Kɛhini is a big ant with a super-foul smell. When your name is Kɛhini, you don't enter the fray when there is a search for the person who just broke wind.

It turned out that Nii Ayi is of the Kɛhinic order. His stool is a stool under stress - being pulled in two directions. With his promise to step down, the other party found its voice. And now as well, Wofa Kapokyikyi has polished up his little Ga Mashie vocabulary and is telling Nii Ayi, "Nii, tɛɛ shie".

A few days ago, Nii Ayi's supporters came out of the Ahenfie to tell us that we don't understand royal speak. And that Nii spoke in proverbs. I used to think that it was only the politicians that thought citizens of Sikaman have *apapransa* in place of grey matter. I have been educated. I was wrong.

The attempted proverbilisation of this plain mayishinated statement by Nii reminded me of the Baba-Jamalian prescription. According to the world-famous Baba-Jamalian principle, when in a position of power, when you see a sheep, it is most appropriate to call it a cow. Afterall, all paintey be paintey.

Meanwhile, we continue to wait for what next adesa would ensue from Adesa We. Ta wɔ adesa, Mensah, ta wɔ adesa.

Wofa Kapokyikyi once told me that when an elder loses respect, even his public fart elicits no response. I still hope not to be fart-neutral where some of our chiefs are concerned.

I hope the Nii Ayi Bonte issue teaches our venerable chiefs to desist from binge-boozing on political akpeteshie. We want to still respect them.

May we never again reach that low montie point. It was the ultimate Yentie Obiaa moment and that is the enduring legacy in my mind with respect to Odekuro.

Till I come your way again with another sebitical, I remain:

Sebitically yours,

Kapokyikyiwofaase

Change In Yaanomship

It was my senior Moshie Dayan who famously declared, when someone tripped him in a fierce fight for a loaf of bread during *scattey* at the dining hall, that "the gbedement of the nuɛ is not the end of his life". The English have a different translation for this, that the downfall of a man does not signify the end of his life. Indeed, this holds true for any venture in which success eludes at any instance. The critical thing is what one does with, and after, such a blip, and whether or not one keeps going. It was Winston Churchill who said that "success is the ability to move from one failure to another without loss of enthusiasm". I call that vim.

Sikaman just entered a new era. There has just been a change in the Ahenfie. The people, subjects no more but citizens, as christened by the new Odekuro, decided to give Odekuro Okasafo Yohani Mahani Nikaboka rest. Behold, we have a new Odekuro!

Odekuro Odieasem Nana Tutubrofo Dankwawura, Wofa Kapokyikyi welcomes you. Wofa says that w'aba a, tena ase.

This was Wofa Kapokyikyi prayer for you as he poured libation at Liberty Fan Club yesterday: "May your reign be peaceful and prosperous. May your reign bring us fruits so big that we will check the size of our posterior orifice before we attempt any swallowing. May the ancestors be with you and grant you wisdom."

I could only nod and say "*Wie!*"

As the change of Odekuro took place, so did the change of Yaanomship. As my friend Rodney Nkrumah-Boateng succinctly captured it, there exists in Sikaman an ancient club called the Yaanomites. They are an old and proud fraternity, fiercely dedicated to the Odekuroship.

Their role and passion are to serve the Odekuro, and they do it best when blindfolded. You wonder how they know who to target when they cover their eyes? Simple. They first group all people into two camps: pro-Yaanom and anti-Yaanom. When a message is received, they first check out the messenger: is he for or against us? When the citizens, not subjects, are in camps, it is easy to volley verbal cannons into the enemy camp. "Are you on the Lord's side?"

The Yaanomites have been mentioned in many of the discussions under trees, especially those that take place when we gather to play dami. It has been said that the Yaanomites were staunch adherents to the Baba-Jamalian principle, also known as Goat-to-Cow, and that their stuffing of their ears with *mmɛfi*[12], making them hard of hearing, contributed to the gbedement of the old Odekuro.

But that is in the past now. The good thing about the Yaanomites is that their ranks are refreshed with the entrance of a new Odekuro. The old Yaanomites then move to a place of purgatory, where one is cleansed of yaanomidity, awaiting whether to become anti-Yaanom or to be yaano-neutral.

So, change has happened and so has the change in Yaanomship. Hail the new Yaanom. Again, Wofa says *mo aba a, mo ntena ase.*

The new Yaanomites didn't have to wait long to get to work. Odekuro's first speech after his enstoolment provided the first shooting practice. It was a good speech, and clearly no one needed elevation to appreciate that fact.

Odekuro Tutubrofo kasa yɛ! The speech was full of both vim and akeshaa, with the right doses of arish-rish. No kontomire. And we hailed and clapped and said "Wiɛ! Tutu bra!"

After the reggae, we play the blues. And it was in the playing of the blues that citizens, not spectators, of Sikaman found

---

[12]The dry fibre from palm nut fruits after the extraction of palm oil and soup, used in the past to deodorise the water pot or cooler.

that some of the reggae of Odekuro's brofo should have been sang with the voice of Bush the Texan who himself had sang the same song done years ago by Woodrow the Wailer. Not our own Ankry the Wailer, who we will discuss one day soon. Such wailing skills cannot be allowed to wallow or wane.

Come and see plenty posts and opinions on plagiarism and copyrights and *thems thems*. Soon, the Yaanomites had to take charge and then we began to see one key evidence of the classic Yaanomated strike: a text being shared on all platforms. The best way to identify such Y-texts is the inscription at the end: "Forwarded as received". It usually tells you the sender doesn't understand the text, hasn't critically analysed it or doesn't really believe it.

And soon enough, there followed the next stage of yaanomstition: *they are against us; they want to pour sand into our gari, they didn't see this in the past.*

Change has come. Tables have turned. And the change of Yaanomship is completed.

But there is hope yet. The principles of Yaanomidity are not cast in stone. The Yaanomites don't need to operate blindfolded. Citizens, not subjects, don't need to be placed in camps. And the old ranking members of the Y-Club don't have to be seen as rabble-rousers.

We have one Sikaman to build. Yaanomites have to quickly hone the skills of separating the palm oil and soup from the mmɛfi, of separating message from messenger and harnessing the collective wisdom of all Sikamanians. It is said that even a faulty wall clock is right twice in a day.

And, oh, when Yaanomites find themselves in a slippery hole, Wofa says they should please stop digging.

Change has come. And, so, some of your old friends will start calling and chatting with you again. Some will start sharing your posts. Some will start hailing you and saying how great your thoughts are.

Don't worry that your posts and viewpoints haven't changed much and wonder why your views suddenly make sense.

Change goes various ways.

Till I come your way again with another sebitical, I remain:

Sebitically yours,

Kapokyikyiwofaase

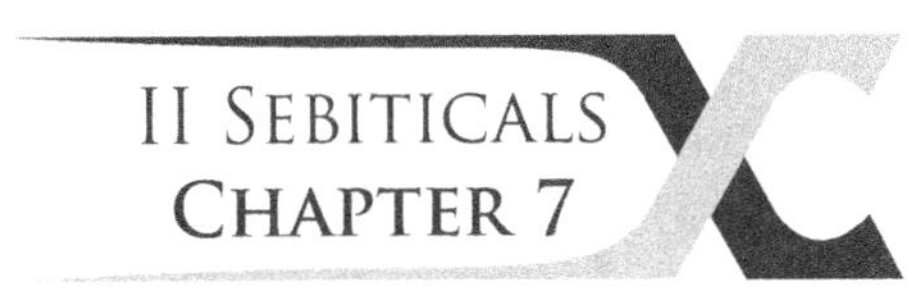

II Sebiticals
Chapter 7

"I Tried It and I Made It"

Dear Wofa Kapokyikyi:

I bring you warm buharattan[13] greetings from Amalaman where the value of cowries here, otherwise known as naiwries, is falling faster than the rate at which Nana Premang Ntow's teeth fell out.

Another big story we are all watching from here is what role Oga Kpatakpata will let Amalaman play in sorting how Papa Jammeh, who drank humble sobolo after losing the bid to extend his time on the throne and then spat it all out, saying that he forgot that he hadn't prepared for his time as an ex-Oga.

You know, Wofa, that Amalaman exported democracy to Sierra Leone when it (Amalaman) had none at home. Sister Charity was definitely not at home. With democracy now in place in Amalaman, Oga Kpatakpata and Amalamanians will

---

[13]Muhammadu Buhari is the President of Nigeria

be more than eager to support the move to uproot Papa Jammeh like a yam.

We watch to see how it goes.

This week, my friend, Abena Krobea, shared the video of a young Malawian inventor called William Kamkwamba. In the video, the young man recounted how famine was ravaging his country in the early 2000s and how he had to drop out of secondary school. Determined to still educate himself, he decided to frequently visit the library of his former school to read books, especially science books. From one of those books, he learnt about windmills, and decided to build one himself. Not having the requisite materials, he visited scrap yards around his house and salvaged bits and pieces of scrap including bicycle parts, and PVC pipes, from which he built his first windmills that powered his house with electricity and also pumped water for irrigation. Awesome stuff! Inspirational!

In this TED talk by William, he made a profound statement: "I tried it. And I made it." He made a move with his ideas; he took a risk on his dreams.

When I watched the video and as I personally tango with the many ideas I have that I haven't tried, knowing what I have to do and yet not doing it, procrastinating, thinking of how to do it perfectly, yet holding back and worrying about the passage of time, giving me a headache, I looked at William and I am provoked to take the pill of action and welcome my relief.

But it is not that easy and that is when I decided to write to you and share my reflections.

At a book reading at Rennie's Garden, Dr Ruby Goka told us that one of the worse things about being a doctor or a medical student is that when one got ill, he or she only imagines the worse of possible illnesses.

Same with the educated African. The educated African seems only to be conditioned for steady state conditions, to feel comfortable only when conditions are certain, and all risks have been fully analysed and covered.

The educated African is the most afraid to take risks on his dreams.

Not so with many entrepreneurs who need to take a plunge into uncertain waters. Not so with William, who tried it and made it.

I am going to try, Wofa.

Many of us are struggling with dreams that are in turbulent state. Unclear about how the dreams will pan out and unsure about whether the dreams are even sensible enough. Like seasoned sailors, like Peter the disciple, we look at the water and the weather and drop anchor, refusing to sail out.

I will sail, Wofa.

The story is told of the rich man whose only daughter fell into a pond infested with crocodiles, at a game reserve. In desperation, as he looked at one giant crocodile close in on his daughter, the rich man shouted for help and promised that whoever could rescue his precious daughter would be given half of his entire wealth. Out of nowhere, one young man dived into the pond, swam quickly and brought the girl out, just in time to miss the closing jaws of the monster crocodile!

After catching his breath, everyone was eager to know from the young man what gave him such confidence.

"Young man," they all asked at once, "what do you have to say about such daring? We all want to know what moved you to dive in. Was it the promised money?"

"Thank you all," he started, "but what I really want to know first is who pushed me!"

I am going to learn to dive, Wofa. Pushed or otherwise.

"I tried. And I made it. Trust yourself. And believe." Those are the words of Kamkwamba.

As I reflect some more, the story of a friend of mine, let's call her Adwoa, come strongly to me. Adwoa was passionate about training and development. She spoke continuously about how she would love to set up an outfit for that purpose when she went out of the company on an expected early retirement. We called it "being paid off". That day never came. One day, Adwoa didn't return to work. She died with her dream.

I am going to find that vim to dive, Wofa. Because, as I told Aboko my friend, sometimes one needs to know when to move before he is pushed. And I have seen a lot of pushing lately. Your company can decide to push you, to sack you. And then you would find that you can actually swim very well and beat crocodiles.

I tried and I made it. William has really provoked me.

Till I come your way another time with another sebitical letter from Amalaman, I remain:

Sebitically yours,

Kapokyikyiwofaase

THE DEPARTURE OF THE J

Kojo Mɛtɛɛ (pronounced *meh-teh*) was a notorious thief in my holy village. It was rumoured that when he entered a room, he could smell exactly where money and valuables had been hidden and go straight for the kill. Or rather, straight for the steal. Those were the days when bank vaults resided in the inner entrails of mattresses, the ones made with straw. When there was fire, mattresses burnt with expensive swag.

One day, my big brother Joe Base, in a bid to protect his savings from Kojo and The Gang, hid his money in such an obscure place that he forgot where he had hidden it! After hours of trying to find it, he gave up and called Kojo, who stepped into the room, closed his eyes, sniffed the air a bit and laughed.

"Bra Joe Base paa, it is under the carpet," he pointed.

Kojo loved stealing the coconuts from the backyard of the local rich man, Opanyin Nemi. He would scale over Opanyin's high wall and climb the coconut trees, plucking the fruits so they fall outside the compound for his gang members to collect. He did so with his eyes looking out for Opanyin, whose single-barreled gun, also called ti aborɛfere (pluck down pawpaw), was feared.

One afternoon, as Kojo was up a coconut tree, he saw perceived movement in Opanyin's house. His friends whistled to warn him but as he craned his neck to investigate, he lost his grip and started falling…

Tum!

Silence…

One of his pals whispered over the wall, they were afraid Kojo was either badly hurt or was dead.

"Kojo Mɛtɛɛ, w'awu anaa?" (Kojo, are you dead?)

The response came in, slowly…

"Minwu yɛ o, na pua na mɛ pua." (I am not dead, but I have been shortened!)

I bring you greetings from Wofa Kapokyikyi, who has been following the issues in The Gambia over the past weeks from his stool at the Liberty Fan Club.

Ei, Wofa said it o. He predicted that Papa Jammeh, like Gbagbo, *baa gbo last show*. Papa Jammeh, like the proverbial fly which didn't listen to advice, has followed the corpse into the grave.

After losing the elections and conceding and dis-conceding, Papa J wanted to copy the senior Papa J but he didn't follow The Handbook well. You negotiate indemnity clauses and transitional provisions before the elections and not after. It was Haillemariam Lemar who said that Jammeh was so sure of winning the Gambian elections that he didn't even attempt to rig it! That surely must explain why Papa J missed the sequence.

Then, he proceeded to dig his feet in. The regional Council of Chiefs said no but only Papa J said yes. Even when his *akyeame*[14] and sub-chiefs said a new dawn had come, Papa J still said the sun was shining brightly on his coast.

One of the key weaknesses of dictators is that they do not realise it when the applause is either gone or it has become faked. They refuse to get it when they lose favour. In leadership, as in life, you need to know when to move before you are pushed.

I always get amused and surprised when African leaders don't want to step down honorably after service. My reason is that we have so few ex-Presidents for the many

---

[14]Akyeame: Linguists

opportunities that exist for such experience in the international community.

That was my position with Gbagbo.

With Papa Jammeh, I am not that clear. Perhaps he analysed that bit, apart from his fear of not resting in peace, and concluded that he is not employable after stepping off the stage as Head of State.

After advising the fly for so long, the regional Council of Chiefs decided to show the corpse to the fly, to let the fly know its potential sleeping partner. The corpse was escorted by soldiers from the land which had carved out a bit of its belly for The Gambia and which almost enveloped the small nation. Other nations, including Sikaman who had ancestral spirits crying for retribution, also provided troops. Amalaman provided iron birds, who could spit fire. These troops started marching "left, right, left, right", singing "O-zami-namina-mina-mina", in that deep voice of the senior Papa J and came knocking on the doors of The Gambia. It was a sight to behold, numbers stretching from the East to the West.

According to the BBC, "The Gambia's entire armed forces are made up of only about 2,500 troops."

Let me sikamanise that for you. The entire Gambian Army will not fill 100 VIP Yutong buses. Our National Theatre and the Conference Centre are all we need to sit the entire army personnel in the Gambia.

The story is told of a new Inspector-General of the Ahenfie police who was informed about some of his men extorting palm wine and cowries from citizens as they returned from their farms. He disguised himself one day and went out to investigate. One of the policemen gave him such a tough time and took all his palm wine at a checkpoint. When he removed his disguise and the policeman recognised him, the junior kotiman saluted clumsily and blurted, "I sack myself, sah!"

When the Chief of Papa J's army saw the multitude of soldiers accompanying the corpse, he weighed his options and stated that the palaver at hand had nothing to do with soldier matter. "I won't commit my men to any stupid fight", he said, and proceeded to take selfies.

Wise man. The toad should not sweat on behalf of the lizard which chews pepper.

Most armies that spend their time terrorising their own citizens spend less time actually preparing to fight real soldiers. I hope the Gambian Army still knows how to fight. You should consider the size of your head before you challenge Etikelenkele to a Head War. When Etikelenkele was a child, he was restrained by his parents from watching birds fly above his head. That act disturbed the equilibrium of his body. His head was that gargantuan.

Wofa Kapokyikyi told me that it was an African proverb that eventually made Jammeh to *jɛ jɛmɛ*.

"It is a Mozambican proverb", he said. "If you want to swallow a mango seed, you first of all calculate the diameter of your anus."

So, I am told that in the heat of the developments, Papa J asked for Teacher Johnson who brought a pair of dividers and took the dimensions of the posterior orifice of the J. It was less than *pi*.

Papa J just gave up.

One of Papa J's main demands for his days outside The Gambia will be the provision of a good washman. Spare a thought for those white gowns. If that request is not met or if the new washman cannot wash with Omo so it shows, Papa J may have to change to khaki gowns. Afterall, our elders say that sankofa is not fatal.

One clear bright news is that the Home-based African Herbalists Association (HAHA) just gained a high-profile permanent member.

Papa Jammeh eventually was uprooted like a seedling. Initially, I wanted him to be uprooted like a yam, but he got lucky. This was a seedling approach.

See, he has been transplanted! *W'apua*! He has been shortened!

I see the Jammeh cloud has a silver lining *paa*. His silly move makes it much much easier for him to be made to account for his atrocities in the past. What he feared – that he would be tried when he handed over – that must have led to this stance, will come on him. On a better platter.

In the end, at the final exit point from The Gambia, Jammeh should be given a ride in a wheelbarrow across the border.

Till I come your way next time with another sebitical, perhaps atop a wheelbarrow, I remain:

Sebitically yours,

Kapokyikyiwofaase

THE ROAD JUST TRAVELLED

In the days of yore when *we were we* and roamed the highlands and low fields of the university of spiritual training, which later was given a coating of the name from Nkroful, there lived an obroni-trained herbalist in the big herbal centre near the road that ran from the abode of Odekuro right into the bosom of Otumfuo[15].

Teacher Croffectus told us many market days ago on the hills of Menya Mewu, which existed side-by-side with the valley of swinging monkeys, that everyone needed to be aware of two aspects of self for life's journeys and to also make decisions on careers: aptitude and attitude; what one's gumption quotient was and what his behaviours and idiosyncrasies inclined him towards.

What Teacher Croffectus failed to add was one's *debiatitude*: how one looks like.

[15]Otumfuo: The King of the Asanti people

This herbalist in the herbal centre near the road looks like a fitter mechanic. Our view in the land of spiritual training was that an obroni-herbalist is supposed to look dadabee kakra, and not to have features that made you look up at the ceiling instead of admiring the handiwork of Odumakoma Nana Nyankonpon. One of the reasons why perhaps Kapokyikyiwofaase didn't even consider the suggestion of Premang Ntow's son, that Premang Ntow's grandson became a herbalist. The debiatitide.

The legend was that during the period when even Nii Saddam reduced the length of his drumming sessions and gave time to the lesser business of reading his books, when men and women alike chewed the midnight kola and burnt the evening osɔnɔ[16], when Sir RED roamed the rooms muttering "minfitɛ gbɛmen average" (I am destroying the cumulative average of students) and admonishing students to draw any line even if they couldn't make head or duna of the isometric drawing questions....during that period of exams, many were those who thronged the herbal centre for some relief from pain and stress, from the toils of preparation for exams and from the stress of not making enough time for one inte or the other, and the repercussions thereof.

The story continues that this fitter-herbalist used to prescribe herbs just as you stated your ailments and many who exited his consulting room found out, when they

[16]Osɔnɔ: Local kerosine lamp

compared tales from not different tails, that they were given the same herbs, even for different complaints. They soon concluded that the herbalist listened only with his hands.

So, one day, Nii Saddam, also called Kule, decided to get to the root of the matter. When he was ushered into the consulting room, he just sat and didn't utter a word. But Fitter-Herbie had started scribbling away and prescribing herbs!

"But you don't even know what is wrong with me!" Kule indicated.

"Ah, but don't you all have the same illnesses and symptoms during this time?" Fitter-Herbie retorted.

I bring you warm greetings from my Wofa Kapokyikyi who told me that whilst it is true what our elders say, that even though heads may look alike, the thoughts in them differ, sometimes when you see how one particularly-shaped head is modeled upon a neck, one can sense that the thoughts in that head have been experienced before in the past, and soon enough, the pouring out of those thoughts confirms the suspicion.

Like the stance of the Fitter-Herbie, many times when one considers the happenings in Sikaman, one gets the feeling of déjà vu, nah, Ghana vu. Many times, the trajectory that issues take, like the path of a quadratic graph that rises and falls, that 'pours water', a line that accelerates to a crescendo and falls, like the crest and trough of a wave, seems too familiar. In Sikaman, many times when the matters hit, one just gets the sense that we have been here just the day, the week, the month or the year before, and one could almost predict the path ahead of the issue.

The steadfast problems of our land never cease, their recycling never come to an end. They are renewed every morning, great is our faithfulness in traversing roads just travelled.

How are our new politicians different from the old? How different do we address our issues? Are our national scripts rehashed just for new actors?

Zimbabwean writer NoViolet Bulawayo wrote a novel entitled *We Need New Names*. Yes, in Sikaman, we need new scripts. We need new ways of doing things. We need new stories. We need new politics. We need to change the narrative. We need new mentalities of citizens. We need different heads and fresh thoughts from these heads, mixing in a national cauldron where each thought acts as an ingredient to produce a national meal of positive progress that delivers tangible development.

We can't continue to be that predictable. We can't continue to peregrinate as if we have no destination as a nation. We must get off the road just travelled and find new paths.

We need new names. No more Ghana vu.

Till I come your way next time with another sebitical, I remain:

Sebitically yours,

Kapokyikyiwofaase

Your State of Being
is Another's Dream

I bring you greetings from Wofa Kapokyikyi who, finding me in a low mood over the past weekend, downloaded one of his choice proverbs. *Me nya wo ayɛ, ɛyɛ musoo*, he told me, meaning that it may be wahala trying to become like someone else. He told me that in life, we all have our races to run, and different roles to play. And for the first time ever, Wofa Kapokyikyi gave me a non-Sikaman quote, using the words of Alexandre Dumas, that "there is neither happiness nor misery in the world; there is only the comparison of one state to another, another more."

I was surprised. I remarked that I didn't know he read many books. He smiled and retorted that *small boys are young*.

I thank you, Wofa.

I spent the weekend of 5 and 6 March 2011 dabbling in two of my delights: spending time with the youth in Cape Coast and ministering with Joyful Way Incorporated in Takoradi, now christened Oil City or Oilkrom.

I was privileged to be invited by Nana Ama Ghansah and her Nhyira Foundation to speak at the Gathering of Visioneers Conference in Cape Coast, bringing together pupils and students from junior high and senior high schools in and around Cape Coast.

It was not all talk, though. We had some good music. On the bill was Michael Oware Sakyi, aka OJ. I had heard a couple of his songs but had neither seen nor heard him live. Two of his popular songs are *Obi Nya W'ayɛ* and *Koso Na Koso*, which he released in 2003. I was impressed with him.

Before singing his last song for the afternoon, OJ shared with us his story, where he had come from, how far God had brought him, how his experiences and desires combined to make him who he had become and provoked our thoughts that God had made each one of us unique. Then he sang *Obi Nya W'ayɛ*, loosely translated from Akan as 'someone wishes he or she was like you'. He asked us to sit quietly and listen to the lyrics. It was good advice.

The story is told of a man, let's call him Kwame Nkrabea, who was so frustrated with life, his lack of success and the non-achievement of his dreams that he decided to end it all. He was broke, in debt, with no hope of recovery. After begging for a few months, he felt he didn't even have the strength to continue begging. One day, he left town to hang himself.

Finding a forest area, Nkrabea selected a tree whose branches were strong enough to ensure the rope held. To delay any chances of his body being found, he decided to remove his clothes, leaving only his underpants. As he tied the noose, he detected some human activity in the undergrowth. With amazement, he saw a man kneeling by his discarded, tattered clothes, carefully folding them, whilst muttering a prayer for a good find.

Nkrabea aborted his suicide mission.

Someone gave a testimony of expressing gratitude and appreciating that his lack of shoes was not that bleak, considering some had no feet. In secondary school, any time I was broke with no food in the chop box, I could thank God that I was able to eat in the dining hall, fresh food, not like the *sopi* boys who came from the nearby villages to help in the pantry so they could go home with the leftover food, what we discarded – actually not much so the *sopi* boys had to sweep the tables to take the crumbs and spills from our plates, literally.

It is good to compare yourself to your peers, to calibrate, so as to encourage yourself to do more. But we should always remember that our paths in life are different. Even twins don't have the same characteristics, a friend reminded me at work this week. Even Siamese twins disagree on what to do from time to time.

As my friend, Dr Bisi Onoviran said, "You shouldn't compare yourself to others; they are more screwed up than you think."

There is always someone who will admire something in you, wishing to be you. Who you are today is someone's dream.

But that is not to say you have to remain at this point. You can only become better from today, as you keep on. But the journey forward is enhanced with a positive appreciation of the path you have trodden, lessons learnt and gratitude of the present. It is only then that you can practise what Eugene V Debs called 'intelligent discontent', which he stated "is the mainspring of civilization". That discontent which says, "I am grateful for what I am, but I can be more".

What is eating you up? Could it have been worse? Reflect and act to improve, to go ahead, to be better.

Till I come your way again with another sebitical, I remain:

Sebitically yours,

Kapokyikyiwofaase

The Tale of Two Mmmms

In the first year after Odekuro Obenfo Yohani Atta Nikanika died, there arose a new Odekuro named Odekuro Okasafo Yohani Mahani Nikaboka, son of Dramaha, who also was a scribe, an Otwerefuo. Odekuro Nikaboka was said to have a friend from the land beyond the cornfields who was as wise as Solomon.

One day, a messenger went crying in the wilderness, proclaiming this special friendship of the mighty one with the wise one and the magicians of the land and all the citizens rose up with one voice asking to know if this friendship was real or that it existed only in the fertile mind of Amakye the town crier. When Agari the chief of the Ahenfie scribes was asked to speak to the citizens on behalf of Odekuro on the said matter, Agari decided to speak to the citizens on behalf of Odekuro before speaking to Odekuro to find out what he should say on Odekuro's behalf.

It came to pass when Agari had spoken to deny any knowledge of Odekuro about the existence even of the temple Solomon built, let alone its builder, there was night and then the day followed.

As each day brings its own wahala, so the next day revealed a new tale from a different tail. Agari the Chief Scribe, having spoken with Odekuro to now ask him what should be said to the magicians and citizens on Odekuro's behalf on the matter, came back to the market square to deliver another version of the tale of the day before, shifting the direction of the story from north to south.

It was then that Wofa Kapokyikyi said his famous words: *whatever Agari says must be allowed to cook for one day and one night.*

Time passed and Odekuro, the son of Dramaha, continued to rule and Agari continued to grow. Soon, the citizens of Sikaman grew weary of the ways of the son of Dramaha and asked him to go tend to his farms and enjoy his days in the arms of the wife of his youth. In his stead, they anointed and installed Odekuro Odiasem Nana Tutubrofo Dankwawura. There was evening and the morning, a new day.

In the morning of the new day, Odekuro Tutubrofo went out hunting for sub-chiefs and deputies and came back with smaller stools to share amongst the chosen few. As per the practice of the traditional council, the names of the called were submitted for consideration by the sub-council appointed by Abrewa to probe the backgrounds and characters of Odekuro's called. The vetting council sat day and night to decide which of the called would be chosen, for had it not been said that many would be called but few chosen?

Wofa Kapokyikyi had told me years ago that the way from the called to the chosen was through a narrow gate and, sometimes, the called tried to lubricate the narrow gates.

So when yesi-yesi started filtering that Egya Arko, son of Boakye (who had been called by Odekuro to man the power house to support the nika-nika of Sikaman) had supplied judicious helping of lubricating oil to ease the joints of the members of the vetting sub-council, all ears were itching for the filla. But it turned out that filla no get legs, na Agari dey carry am.

Wofa sent me out to get him the full rundown, which I did with alacrity. I didn't have to go far. I met Ziboyo behind the Ahenfie, who told me that the summary of the matter is this:

Agari said Munchinga said *yesi* Joe Wise says *yesi* Egya Arko gave Joe Wise the lubricating oil to give to Munchinga to give to Agari and his friends so they could keep wide open the narrow gates so Egya Arko could pass on to the glory of the chosen few.

A good case study of Yesi-Yesi?

When I told Wofa Kapokyikyi, he repeated that if Agari was involved, then thawing was required. There was evening and the morning, a new day.

In the morning of the new day, Joe Wise went shouting from the rooftops that he didn't give any lubricating oil to Munchinga. The entire village was confused.

When Agari was asked whether he was sure it wasn't Jay Wise he was referring to, instead of Joe Wise, he clarified that he dealt with neither Jay Wise nor Jay Wise, but rather with Munchinga and that only Munchinga could tell who the source of the lubricating oil was. The chorus was unanimous: "We want Munchinga! We want Munchinga!"

When Munchinga, who had just woken up from a deep sleep and was rushing to a funeral at Ankosia, was asked whether he had received any lubricating oil from Joe Wise, he said '*Walahi-talahi*!' and swore by Allah the Magnificent that he hadn't even seen lubricating oil in his entire life. The confusion became *basaaa*!

When Odekuro was informed about the basaacious commotion that was brewing in the Sikamanian pot, he went into a conclave with Abrewa and the Tufuhene. The steaming pots that were brought to the entrance of the Ahenfie, just before the three - Odekuro, Abrewa and

Tufuhene - exited from the inner chamber, gave a hint of the decision that had been taken. The Tufuhene confirmed it a few minutes later: a ko-num-tee was set up to drink some tea and deliberate on the palaver.

More thawing time. There were many evenings and many mornings. And market days came and went.

The morning of the new day after many evenings, the verdict of the ko-num-tee was declared to the entire village by Amakye the town crier, as follows:

The metemetemism of a rumour does not metamorphose a rumour into fact.

The ko-num-tee said Agari had indulged in yesiyesimisms and found him guilty of ko-num-tempt. When I asked Wofa Kapokyikyi what that meant, he said it meant Agari attempted to drink some of the tea from the chambers of the ko-num-tee. I was even more confused.

But just as I tried to seek clarification, Efo Dogbevi, the letter-writer who lives at Anloga, who was passing by, overheard our conversation and asked Wofa Kapokyikyi a question, as follows: "Wofa, if a cat steals fish, another cat accuses him of that act and the accused cat denies it, leading to a committee of fish-loving cats being set up to investigate...do you expect the committee of cats to publish a report that confirms that cats love fish?"

I don't remember what Wofa Kapokyikyi said in response. What I remember was only that Wofa asked me, when Efo had left, whether Efo was also part of the CATholics.

I could only turn to my favourite book: the Book of Nahum. And say *hmmm*.

Till I come your way again, with some chinginga to soothe my confusion, I remain:

Sebitically yours,

Kapokyikyiwofaase

ONCE UPON A POST SO HIGH

Once upon a time, in the land of KwaMan, the natives of the Bibiman forest decided to hold a drinking and thinking bout with their counterparts in the forest across the Talantic river, called Bronikrom. After all, didn't the elders say that *yε nom nsa, na yε fa adwen?* Truly, as we drink, we think at the same time.

Considering that it has been long decided that alternating venues was a good idea, the leaders of both forests decided to hold the drink-think session in Bronikrom. Also, due to the long distance between the two forests, the herdsmen of each Bibiman tribe were selected to go on this journey.

However, there arose from the tribe of Bongo a man crying in the wilderness, questioning and lamenting. The Man from Zeh family of the tribe of Bongo wondered whether the food in Bibiman was not enough to feed the herdsmen from the two forests, whether the hamlets of Bibiman were not worthy enough to house the Bronikromers and whether enough Bibimanian houses and donkeys could not be marshalled to take the natives of Bronikrom around during the drinking and thinking festival.

"Is this rocket science or common sense? Or something I am missing?" the man from the Zeh family of the tribe of Bongo concluded.

All of Bibiman listened and nodded and wondered, not for the first time, where the Zeh man got his wisdom from. Efo Dogbevi was the first to respond: that the love of borborbor precipitated such wisdom from the innermost parts of a man. Teacher Johnson added that it could be the Zeh man's love for nsempiisms. Obaapanyin Potisaa said it was rather the nectar from the serwaanic well that was making the Zeh man so bold, especially in the year when the entire universe was singing 'Be Bold!'.

As the Bibiman still reflected in silence, a loud voice, with a high pitch, rose from the heart of the forest. Eyes and heads turned. Few ears could recognise this voice and not many eyes could recollect this face. But his words were to enter the book of legends.

Wofa Kapokyikyi was one of the few who indicated that they knew the owner of the voice and told me that the man was from the Kwa family of the tribe of Meh, from an old family of high priests.

The Kwa man delivered his high words and also wondered why after many years of waiting with serwaanic patience, the Zeh man didn't hold his return to Bongo to receive the daughter of his father-in-law and swim in the Tonga river of Bongo. The Kwa man wondered whether the kofi brokeman along the banks of River Bongo were not fit for the guests at his nuptial festival and whether the canoes on River Bongo were not deemed worthy to cater to the transport needs of his guests.

"Is this rocket science or common sense? Or something I am missing?" the man from the Kwa family of the tribe of Meh concluded.

Again, all of Bibiman heard and nodded, and wondered whether the men of the Kwa family were related to the Zoom-Zoom.

But as Bibiman reflected in silence, a chemical reaction was slowly taking place. It turned out that according to the laws of *manasematics*, a punch delivered on social media in the presence of trolls and enabled by the magic of screenshots underwent a chain reaction into a high post.

This was a very high post, which flew high and was shared by many high people who were either high on admiration or on payback vim. My friend, Egya Free Tong who changed his name to Jeffrey Tong when he was baptised by the catechist, put it more sebitically, stating that the post "flew high with the banner of nsempiism across the Talantic oceans and beyond". Which is true, because when the goat was using its backside to spread semi-solid effluent on the walls of the houses in the village, its posterior was also getting painted. In this high post-erio-painting, the nsempiic cover of the nkrataa that Kapokyikyiwofaase penned was an unintended beneficiary.

Many years ago, on the hills of Menya Mewu, a boy who had just arrived in the school that Osagyefo built was asked what his favourite food was. He hadn't been around too long to know that the delicacies from his village didn't sound too well in the city and needed some *brofolisation*[17] when being mentioned. Same reason why Nii Okaitey responded to the same question by saying that his favourite food was corn balls in tweed jacket on a plate of calamari with ogyemma sauce and a guard of honour of sliced shallots. This other boy wasn't that suave yet. He said his favourite meal was brɔdze dwow (what the Fantis call roasted unripe plantain). His friends started calling him Brɔdze Dwow. But this boy was a fast learner. He decided not to protest the name and fight the teasing. With time, his nickname was upgraded to Brɔdze J and by the time he got to the senior stage of his education, everyone was calling him Senior BJ.

It was on the Menya Mewu Hills that Kapokyikyiwofaase discovered that a tease should expect to be teased. Learning

[17]To anglicise (one's name)

to manage your period under teasing fire was part of the game of learning teasing ropes. To ride the crest and manage the trough and glide the waves.

But this strategy was not employed by the Zeh man who decided to shoot from the trough. And the Kwa man countered again.

The KwaMan trajectory then went through block factories, radio studios, Zuckerberg deactivations, back alleys and front alleys. Until the next big thing happened in Sikaman when, as usual, the KwaMan saga was thrown under the conveyor belt that brought the next saga.

Oseeey, Sikaman!

Meanwhile, somewhere in Sikaman, a manager of a celeb is planning to rent a Nana Kwame to deliver a high comment so the celeb can block to follow a KwaMan trajectory. Not a bad idea but this is what Wofa Kapokyikyi says: not all animals can run and not be classified as crazy. Indeed, not all celebs who bring their hands close to their heads are called Abodam.

Wofa Kapokyikyi is also drinking and thinking; after all, he is also a person! As for me, I know no rocket science and I am still searching for common sense.

But the Kwa man's response to the second epistle of the Zeh man had me muddled. He wrote, thus: "Your response fit (sic) into fundamentalist theories of epistemic justification".

Eish!

So, let me ask a common man's question o. What is the best way to understand this second response: rocket science or common sense? Or is there something I am missing?

Till I come your way again with another sebitical, I remain:

Sebitically yours,

Kapokyikyiwofaase

II SEBITICALS
CHAPTER 13

SIKAMALIAMENTARY PALAVA

I bring you very foamy greetings from the shed of Akwasi Sorfree, the best palm wine tapper in Wasaman, where, departing from his regular practice, Wofa Kapokyikyi is having a calabash of palm wine. He told me that from time to time, even Memuna gets tired of fula. No Liberty Fan Club visits today.

Wofa was quite pensive today. Me, I just sat and enjoyed the conversations around the benches under the shed.

"A fool in a pensive mood is not making any judicious plans; he is still a buffoon," Wofa whispered, almost to himself.

"Ei, Wofa Kapokyikyi! Please explain." I had no inclination what he meant by that.

"My son, a rich man who becomes poor is still better than a poor man who is trying to become rich."

"Ei! As for today, you are really swimming in parables."

Wofa was not done. "A mad man who gets cured still has some tricks with which to frighten children. And a fool who is assumed wise only has to open his mouth to clear any doubts."

I had to get closer to Wofa Kapokyikyi to confirm whether he was in the spirit. He wasn't. He was sober, which was even more dangerous. For what a man says when drunk, he thought about whilst sober, and Wofa's thoughts, when being cooked in his fertile mind, were caustic.

Oh yes, I bring you greetings from Wofa Kapokyikyi, who told me that Kotei, the jack-of-all-trades, who recently graduated from village electrician to cable TV fixer, has finally come to install the apotowiwa on top of his roof so that his television set can now receive images from the capital.

Wofa says he has been following the proceedings, news, discussions, accusations, fights and all the drama from the House of State this year, and his mind was still trying to manage all the twists and turns.

"I love the state of our Parliament now. For every story, there are about four versions of the *near truth*. And then the truth. I love it more when each storyteller calls the other a liar. Makes it even more colourful when the lied to is not believed, when he states his version of the truth, which cannot be distinguished from the lies which the liar tries to discount."

"Ei, Wofa, son of Premang Ntow and grand nephew of Bassanyin!" That was all I could say. I started to think that the palm wine wasn't getting on well with the physiological mechanisms of my Wofa's metabolism.

It is getting tangled and mangled and appearing far from simple, eh? It is sounding convoluted and you are getting discombobulated, eh?

Exactly! That's the idea, to make you appreciate my confusion with the train of thoughts that Wofa was peregrinating today.

"You see, my wofaase, our big men in the House of State have given onto themselves the 'Insult Privilege'. They have arrogated to themselves alone the power to disrespect MPs. To insult MPs. To fight MPs. They say to the ordinary people, 'You have no right to disrespect us or to speak ill of us. We don't need your help. We can do it ourselves. To one another.' Who am I to disagree?"

Wofa paused and took a sip from his calabash. The foam formed a white line above his upper lip. I wondered how that line would have formed if Wofa had an Andamic[18] moustache. He didn't give me much time to wonder.

[18]Named after Professor Kwesi Andam, late Vice Chancellor of Kwame Nkrumah University of Science and Technology, who was famed for his thick moustache

"You remember the accusations and counter accusations about the black polythene courier bags? You remember the naadoli-cowric statement that was covered with a polythene sheet? Did you see the fight that brought us good memories of the zoom-zoom days?"

I nodded. I did remember all of them, I answered.

I asked Wofa if the continuous use of the Insult Privilege wouldn't dent the image of Parliament.

He chuckled.

"How can you dent further a milk tin that has been used for various rounds of *chaskele*[19]?" He said this slowly, nodding slowly.

He was done with his palm wine. Just one calabash. He stood up and held one of the bamboo pillars holding the roof of the shed in place.

Amakye, the town crier, who was sitting across us and had his transistor radio glued to his ears, just increased the volume as we heard the latest news from the House of State. The voice from the radio said some big men of the house had used their special nkrataa to take some people across the cornfields and left them there. The radio voice said the man

---

[19] A local bat-and-ball (stick-and-ball) game played between two teams of two players. It is a Ghanaian game played by children and it is like cricket. The ball is made with a crushed tin can and a suitable narrow plank of wood or stick is used as a bat.

making the accusation was called Jon. Not John o, not any of the former Odikros.

We all said "*Hmmmm*".

Except Wofa, who said "*Oyiwa*[20]!"

"Did you notice that, in the visa matter of Jon vs the MP4 (apologies to Efo Kofi Gbedemah)," Wofa asked, beginning to walk towards the police station junction, at which we would turn left towards home, "only *nieces* and *wives* were carried along, and not nephews or brothers?"

I followed him down the road, with my mind made up on one thing: palm wine is not good for my Wofa Kapokyikyi.

Till I come your way again, hopefully when Wofa Kapokyikyi reverts to sampling the normal spirits at the Liberty Fan Club, I remain:

Sebitically yours,

Kapokyikyiwofaase

---

[20]Exclamation. An adulteration of the expression 'There you are!'

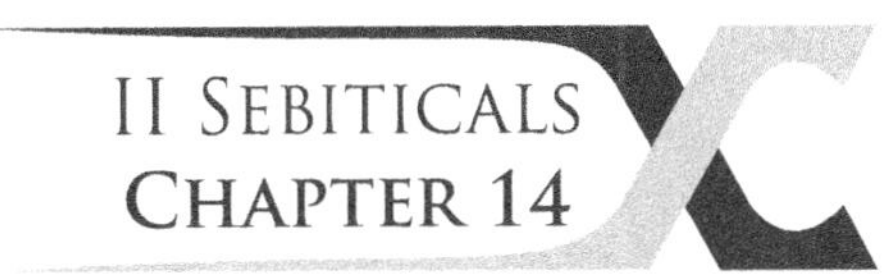

II Sebiticals
Chapter 14

Have You Seen
the Gyata[21] You Reared?

There is a popular cartoon that has been making the rounds for years.

Let me describe the progression in the scene for you.

The scene opens with actor standing in front of the cage with the lion locked behind it. The director briefs the actor that when the 'action' cue was given, the actor is to open the cage and free the lion. The lion will chase the actor around as the actor acts scared and distressed. The director then assured the actor that he shouldn't worry about the lion harming him.

"Don't worry,' the director said, 'the lion won't eat you. It is written here in the script."

[21]Twi for lion

"All well and good,' the actor replied, "you might have written the script, but the question is, 'Has the lion read the script too?'"

In the run-up to the 2016 elections in Sikaman, the current governing party trained some *gyatas* and got some actors to go to town with those gyatas. It is clearer by the day that not everyone read the script.

Sebitically speaking, the NPP is reaping the results of its militarization in the run-up to the last elections. I pray that what is happening with the Delta, Invisible Forces, Azorka Boys, Kandahar Boys and associated vigilante lions, which have grown from cubs, will be a lesson for the future.

As I reflected on the journey to this place of violence, I realised that it is only the unobservant who would say where we are is as a result of magic. There was a build-up, gradually. At least, I saw it. And going through my previous posts on social media, I found quite a number of signposts.

In May 2015, I had a short exchange on a friend's page who called foot-soldiers of NDC the "most useless" she had ever known. I retorted that all political foot-soldiers in Ghana are useless, including those of the NPP. The propensity for foot-soldier nonsense is no respecter of party colours.

I asked her not to worry if she disagreed with me on my assertion as I didn't intend to convince her. You see, one doesn't need to use words to convince anyone about the characteristics or potential shenanigans of foot-soldiers; the foot-soldiers themselves will, by their deeds and utterances.

So, after that, we entered the season of the foot-soldiers as the parties started their primaries. My friend was soon impressed.

In the run-up to the last elections, I made a statement on my Facebook wall that ruffled not a few feathers. On 25 March 2016, I wrote:

"I have observed a trend over the past few years. The NPP is trying very hard to shed off its middle-class, book-long tag and to show that it can also talk rubbish and meet the NDC boot-for-boot. Gloves are off. The NDC is trying very hard to remove the rural, mass, rough and violence-inclined tag and appeal more to the middle. Gradually, the NPP is resembling the NDC of old and the NDC is resembling the NPP of old."

I leave you to judge how this has played out. You be the judge.

My only comment is that the gloves were never put back on. The vigilantes are knocking their masters with ungloved fists. And in the gut too.

The previous year, on 15 May 2015, I had this from an excursion in my mind:

"What do the teeming semi-literate, usually unemployable and mostly irrational foot-soldiers of our political parties want from their inordinate support for their parties? And from the victories of their parties? The answer to that should lead you some sober reflections. That has a great impact on the quality of the output from our political leadership. And on what we achieve as a nation between election campaigns."

A few days later, on 21 May 2015, I wrote: "The foot-soldier nonsense has started in the NPP."

On 7 November 2015, I quoted the Communications Director of the NPP in a post as follows:

"'We haven't done a good job of teaching tolerance to our party supporters...' Nana Akomea. Very poignant. This phenomenon of party foot-soldiers. It will bring us some big wahala one of these days. Soon."

Party foot-soldiers have seized toilets, constituency party offices, party officers, national party offices; burnt party offices, chased district chief executives out of their offices, stormed court premises, turned into pseudo-armies and continue to enjoy political support.

On 7 February 2016, I wrote on my #QuotesbyNAD page: "This foot-soldiers-going-on-rampage-at-will nonsense must be stopped. One day, they will have nothing else to vandalise but their leaders who fail to call them to order today."

That day is precariously close.

One day soon, these same party foot-soldiers will seize the Jubilee House and seize the President.

We have already seen the back-and-forth with the court case involving the Delta Forces 1 & 2 teams.

In *Arrow of God*, Chinua Achebe wrote that the man who brings home ant-infested firewood should not complain when lizards start to visit. According to Nana Ampadu, in his song *Woyoo woyoo*, a leopard who goes on a pilgrimage to Mecca doesn't turn into a vegetarian. Even if he becomes head of a *masalachi*[22].

What we are experiencing with the vigilante groups in the NPP follows the principles of Newton's First Law of motion, which states that every object will remain at rest or in uniform motion in a straight line unless compelled to change its state by the action of an external force. When a car is in motion, the occupants travel at the speed at which the car is moving. When the car stops, the objects in the car (including the occupants) still travel at pre-stop speed of the

---

[22]Islamic basic school

car. Unless an external force changes their state, and restraints them. Like a seat belt.

The vigilante groups are still travelling at pre-elections and pre-inauguration speed. The governing party, their party, needs to find restraints to keep them in check and change their state. As quickly as possible.

This gyata who has even seen the Promised Land is asking for barbecued officials for dinner. With a serving of sobolo[23].

The feeding of foot-soldiers has emboldened them to go out to hunt for themselves. Soon, if unchecked, this reared gyata will break loose and start chewing live meat.

Till I come your way with another sebitical, I remain:

Sebitically yours,

Kapokyikyiwofaase

---

[23]Ghanaian name for a drink made of rosella leaves, it is referred to with different names in different countries where the drink can be found, but it is generally referred to as Bissap.

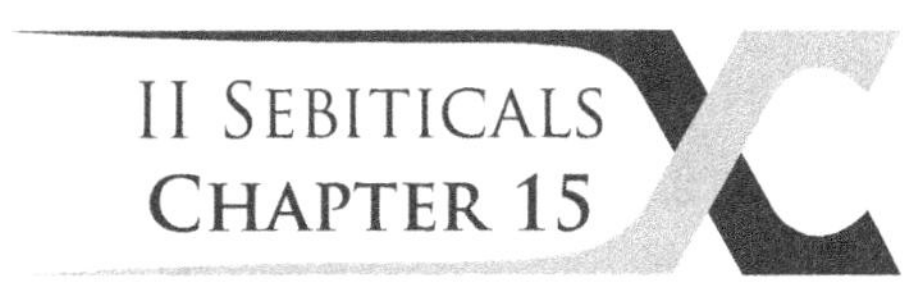

A PROFILING ENCOUNTER

Dear Wofa Kapokyikyi,

I haven't felt this insulted and angry in a long while.

I am on my way to Athens, today 10 September 2016, via Paris on Air France. At the pre-check in counter, where verification of documents is done at Murtala Mohammed Airport, the Nigerian lady indicates that the Schengen visa from the Greek embassy is not allowed on the airlines (KLM/Air France) if the holder hasn't travelled to a Schengen country before. She flips through my two passports that I handed over to her. She suggested that they would have to "off-load" me and proceeded to start filling the appropriate form for that purpose. She told me she just finished off-loading one such passenger.

I said, "Oh wow!"

She asked where I work and I tell her and provide all the supporting documents including company ID and letter of invitation from our sister company in Greece, which stated my designation. I then showed her my UK student visa, which is in my first passport (in another pack of two older passports), asking her if a travel to the UK mattered. She took pictures of all these and send to their chat forum on WhatsApp, awaiting further directions. At this point, it was all civil as I expected her to trigger their standard procedures and seek approval for my boarding.

Then she looked at my bag (1 piece, 24kg) whilst the allowance is 2 pieces. She let out what got me annoyed:

"Your bag is too big for someone going for only 10 days. It looks like a bag for someone who is not coming back."

I blew my top!

"I consider it an insult," I told her calmly, surprising myself. I was boiling inside; the heat of my anger could have easily cooked beans.

She said that is how they 'profile' and that they were there to profile.

Profile? I thought that was a term used by people we called racists, on blacks. I thought that was a word peculiar to the

US, especially lately with all the news we have been hearing. I asked her whether she knew what I was carrying and why one bag was too big for ten days when the allowance was for two anyway?

"If you are going for a vacation, yes; but not for a business meeting."

She wasn't making sense anymore. I know when to stop when an argument is going nowhere.

She left to go upstairs to process passengers for the final boarding and told me her other colleague will attend to me. Eventually, I was called, and I completed the check-in procedures. I also called the company airport passages guy who I like to swerve when I travel, not seeking to worry him as I travel through the Lagos airport often so quite at home. He was livid!

We just don't respect ourselves as African, as Blacks.

After I submitted my dissertation and, thus, finished my Master's in the UK on the 15 September 2006, I stayed in the UK for just two more weeks. This was because I opted to serve as a Student Assistant for Nottingham University's International Welcome Week, where the University helps freshers to settle in and go through induction. I was back in Ghana on 2nd October and resumed work in November. I returned to the UK in December to graduate and returned right after graduation, to continue working in Ghana and on the continent (with a month to spare on my student visa).

This was in line with my cardinal belief that I don't have to sweat elsewhere, as I wrote in my book *I Speak of Ghana*, where I stated "Why sweat my youthful years away building someone's village and not mine? Why put my shoulders to a wheel that turns another economy whilst the one that has my umbilical cord tied to it travels south? And in returning to Ghana, I was returning to Africa, to the continent that needs the resources to grow. How can Africa improve if we don't want to stay, sweat and swim against the tide of under-development and turn our economies around? Why sweat elsewhere when I can sweat on the continent, and stay in a better Ghana, a better Nigeria, a better Africa?"

I haven't travelled back to UK since then, mainly because work hasn't sent me there. And many of my friends know I hardly do non-business travel, especially outside Africa, because I absolutely hate the notion that a visa officer would think I wish to be an illegal immigrant and ask questions we as Africans wouldn't ask when his kin and kind wish to visit the continent.

So, for a fellow African to think that a professional, an engineer, an expatriate in a multinational company in another African country would want to travel to Europe only to escape Africa was a painful insult.

Even a low-grade airport official, who may not have travelled before (sorry if I am profiling her too), thinks that a professional engineer has nothing to do with his life but to run away to Europe via Athens and live as an illegal immigrant.

At the pre-departure check point, she tried to be nice and smiled and wished me a safe trip. I didn't mind her.

"You didn't respond to my wish," she whispered.

I gazed at her and didn't even blink.

I don't forget those who insult me.

I may take condescension from someone different and put it down to ignorance and bigotry but not from a fellow black.

This experience, aside the annoyance, caused me to think deeply on the flight. How do I contribute to build my country and continent such that no one, not even our own selves, would think about fleeing from the continent at the least opportunity? How do I help to change the narrative?

It took less than five minutes for the immigration guy to stamp my passport at the Paris Charles de Gaulle Airport to go to the boarding gate to Athens.

He started in French, and, once again, I missed my French teachers, including Mr Howusu, who is remembered mostly for his lashes and the rice and stew his wife sold to the student than any conjugation he managed to get us to do.

"Parle Anglais?" I responded, adding some gestures for effect. He thankfully changed to broken English.

"*Where you going?*" he asked. I told him.

"*How many times you go there?*"

"Huh? Only one time," I responded, mirroring his level of English proficiency.

"*How many times? How many times you spend there?*"

Got it! "Seven days," I responded.

And that was it. I was in the Schengen zone.

At Athens, no one asked for any passport checks. Apparently, once in the zone, an intercity and inter-country flight is like a domestic flight. How nice.

No profiling.

Seems some can be more French than Jacques Chirac.

Till I come your way again with another sebitical, not from Athens but from Amalaman, I remain:

Sebitically yours,

FROM MY SEBITICAL COUCH – VGMA 2017

The Vodafone Ghana Music Awards (VGMA) for 2017 (covering the performance year of 2016) was held on 8 April 2017 at the Accra International Conference Centre. As an avowed *old duade*[24] who has over the years drifted away from the path of current music trends and the new school genres, some of which I don't understand and many of whose artistes I don't know, I do not have the habit of staying up to watch the typically long program that runs into the early hours of the following day, usually not starting on time.

The best I do, in the past years, has been to 'watch' the program on Facebook (mostly) and Twitter, following the posts of dedicated members of CAG – Couch Analysts of Ghana, whose witty commentaries from the red carpet moments to the moment when the top award – Artiste of

[24]Older person, seen by the millennials as not up to date with current trends

the Year – is awarded, makes for better entertainment than the program itself. Notable members of CAG are Kwame Gyan, Kofi Obirikorang, Andre Jnr, Francis Doku (he is normally off duty on VGMA days as he attends in person and could be relied upon for inside information), Nuerki Ata-Bedu, Lawrencia Elikem Zigah, Prosper Afuti, Kofi Yankey and Ayimadu Bekoe.

I was planning to follow the same path this year. Until I checked a WhatsApp message from my friend Kwabena Poku, which indicated that the show would be telecast live on DSTV, which meant Kapokyikyiwofaase, the Old Duade, could also watch from Amalaman and show fellow Duades like the MP of Facebook South, Hon. Rodney Nkrumah-Boateng, that duades move by sizes.

Predictably, during the build-up to the show, old duades like Rodney and Prof HKP were asking what VGMA meant. Rodney said it stood for 'Very Good Men Abound' and Matthew Ayiku wondered if it was a contraceptive. Well, you now know who influenced the new way of pronouncing VGMA. Vagima, is it? These Old Duades will *kill me shy*! See, the best pitch you can make to an Old Duade, when helping him to understand what the VGMA stands for, is to tell him that it is the ECRAG Awards. ECRAG stands for the Entertainment Critics and Reviewers Association of Ghana. At one point, it was ACRAG. More on that later.

For the red-carpet session, what first hit me was the Red Sea dress. Then I saw a train, actually lots of trains. Frankly, the trains had it. My humble view was the red train of the Red Sea should have on wheels and a barricade put around it for safety purposes. I loved the fact that most of those questioned on whom they were wearing (apart from themselves) mentioned designers (the old duade terms are tailors and seamstresses) in Kumasi et al. A good showcase of our pride in our own. My best red-carpet moment was when Nana Ama McBrown appeared. She comes across to me as so real, someone who takes life easy and makes the most of it, enjoying every moment.

As Elikem the Tailor (shouldn't it be Designer, as in current-speak or is it bespoke-speak?) and Berla Mundi (yeah, forget that it was my first time of seeing her name) rounded up the red carpet session, it occurred to me that I hadn't actually seen any red carpet. Many of the CAG members put my intrigue to rest: they indicated that this year, it was decided that one of the red-carpet hosts should wear the red carpet.

Then we were cued in for the program itself to start. And, I got my first major disappointment. We lost the feed. For a couple of hours. What a missed opportunity to showcase Ghanaian music to the entire continent and to show we have also arrived. I lost a lot of vim due to that, but how for do? As we waited, the CAG members went back to their previous red-carpet posts and expanded them. We needed to keep busy.

Fortunately, the feed was restored, and I got back onto my sebitical couch. As you would see as you read on, I didn't attempt to do a critical assessment of songs and genres and awards. It is clear that I am not qualified. There is a limit to which a duade can act as 'youthe' (apologies to the Katanga folks). So, I will share a few thoughts of the performances and some reflections from the past, as to how we can improve the industry.

First of all, the program ran for too long. Far too long. Did I hear that this year's event was to be quite efficient? It must have run for at least five hours. We should improve that.

The performances are not well-rounded. These are shows and must be choreographed. The big stage was not fully utilized and many of the performers looked isolated on stage. After the first two or three acts, I admitted, reluctantly, to myself that my time had indeed passed. I couldn't even catch the words of the songs. Then Becca performed. At least I knew her songs. Then Kinaata got me with his T'adi Fante. There is something just exotic about T'adi[25] Fante in songs. *Naadze naadze*. Reason why I still miss TH4Kwagees. Okay, you got the duadeness vibe, forgive me.

Charles Amoah and Naa Amanua lifted the game for me. It was clear Charles Amoah rehearsed with the band. Even the band came to life! What energy! Performance! You know what they say about old wine and taste, right? But, in there, I

---

[25]Takoradi, a city in Ghana

wondered how come our highlife stars seem to have "better" longevity compared to our hiplife stars. Many of our hiplife and new stars just come to pass, as it were.

Stonebwoy was good. Even before I started listening to him, just from his appearance, it was evident Stonebwoy had scripted and rehearsed his act. That's performance. Even though I didn't get any of the words he didn't sing in the Ga language. I guess I have to brush up on my *patois*. Sarkodie was great and I was gladdened by the young ones he sang with; more on that later. My revelation of the evening was the young Kwame Eugene.

From many of the performances, it seemed to me that many of these new artistes sing only in the studios and do not do any further voice training and practice. It shows when they sing outside studios. And they felt uncomfortable or out of sorts on the performance stage. Mastery of the stage is not learnt on big stages. It is learnt on the circuit, and even off stage. Many of our young artistes need to work on their craft. Work it!

On the production itself and the telecast, the visuals and sounds were not synchronized. Felt like an 80s Chinese movie. Was the theme for the stage design inspired by some science fiction cum space travel sort of thing?

The moment when the deceased actors and actresses were remembered was touching. May the departed stars rest in peace.

Charterhouse, the event organisers, seemed to have briefed the presenters of the awards to say "...and the nominees are..." and then the video rolls. They should be told that when you use such a leader in a statement, the subsequent sentence must flow and make sense. Well, the video starts with "...the Vodafone...blah blah..." Not kosher. Next time, if using the same style for videos, the presenters should rather be briefed to ask for the video of nominees to roll, for example, "...shall we now get to know the nominees?"

I stayed up paa, I did. But, in the end, the duadeness of a man cannot be hidden under the bushel. I fell asleep two awards from the ultimate. I woke up about 20 minutes later and made a post of congratulations to Joe Mettle, who made history by being named Artiste of the Year, the first one in the gospel genre.

After all, I could always blame my delayed post on the epileptic nature of Amalaman networks and the dry-season-tv-ness of DSTV.

So I said I would not say anything about the classification of awards but just allow an old duade this one. After all, old age must be respected, no? My friend Andre Jnr brought my mind to the classification of Kinaata's Confession as highlife. I was confused too, but I took it that the definition of highlife has changed when I wasn't paying attention. If I were thinking the same as the 'youthe' Andre, then perhaps I can safely brag to Hon. Rodney that, within the Duadepacy, there are ranks; there are duades and then there are High Duades, anaa? Duade bi twa duade mu!

Back to how old duades would relate to the VGMAs and how we used to experience music awards in the days when we were we, my mind again went to ECRAG and I wondered, again, why we are unable to sustain some of the brilliant nurturing and apprenticeship programs we had in the past. For instance, I am attempting a review by this write-up. In the days of yore, one could rely on the reports of professional critics who had gone through mentoring and training. Indeed, the critics and reviewers were the ones who organised the awards. I remember stalwarts like Uncle Nanabanyin Dadson, under whose tutelage Francis Doku developed. What happened to ECRAG? For sure, we have entertainment writers now; but do we have critics and reviewers?

On the subject of apprenticeship, and on my disappointment with the quality of performances, I thought again of how the highlife legends we have today were nurtured by those before them. For instance, Akwasi Ampofo Adjei aka Mr. AAA, Dada Thick, the Shining Star, who passed away in 2004 and is acknowledged as one of the biggest names in Ghana's highlife genre, trained and mentored similarly big names in Ghana's music industry today such as Abrantie Amakye Dede, the founder and leader of Apollo High Kings International, Ali Baba of Mahu Odo Anya Shock fame, K. K. Kabobo and Cudjoe, popularly called Papa Shee, who was one of his dancers. Just an example. Nana Ampadu had in his stable many young singers who grew up into their own. The young learnt from the old and then detached to develop their own nests. I am gratified to know that Sarkodie has under his wings some young artistes like Strongman, whose punchline "Mi rap gyina Circle s ashawo" got me blinking twice! This morning, my friend Kobby Blay sent me a link for the Trumpet song and I learnt that Sarkodie featured Medikal, Strongman, Koo Ntakra, Donzy and Pappy Kojo. We need more of those. Apprenticeship of the young under the old.

We must build an industry with collaboration and not beefs, whatever that means.

From my sebitical couch in Amalaman, this has been Kapokyikyiwofaase reporting for the Sikaman News Agency.

AN ECCLESIASTICAL PAULOGUE TO THE MANASONIANS

In the first year of the reign of Odekuro Odieasem Nana Tutubrofo Dankwawura, there were rumours and reports of malfeasance in the corridors of the temple. When asked for the meaning of the word 'malfeasance', the scribes of the land explained that it was the situation where the incense from the burnt offerings had malodor. One of the major scribes, a man from the Manasonians, took upon himself to open the windows into the temple so both Jews and Gentiles alike would sniff the nunu scent and testify.

Meanwhile, many years before Odieasem ascended the throne, there was born a man known as Saul. This Saul later attended the institute of high learning in Rome and was introduced to Plato, Aristotle, Descartes, Kant, Hegel, Schopenhauer, Nietzsche, Marx and Socrates. He also learnt the ways of Sulla, Julius Caesar and Marcus Aurelius. Right from the high tower, he took a garment of pure Scottish fabric and, with letters from the bearded philosophers of the land, set off to uphold the virtues of the Universe.

One day, on his way to Okponglomascus, suddenly a voice sounded around him and a light flashed.

The voice called out: "Go ye towards the road to Fanoafa and ye shall be told what to do."

In Fanoafa lived a disciple of the Brand, a Sammenitan called Sam-Hatta. The word came to him: "Go out on the Fanoafa road and ye shall find a young man in Scottish garb, who ye shall take onto thy fold; for he is my chosen instrument to build and sustain the Brand."

Picking up his rod, Sam-Hatta the Sammeritan went forth by the Way of Avenor and took the long road towards Okponglomascus where he met Saul. Then Sam-Hatta, the man of Sammenria, held the hands of Saul and blessed him, saying, "Brother Saul, ye have been found worthy of the Brand and selected by the Voice; the Voice that spoke to you on the Okponglomascus road has directed me to you, so you might be imbued with dumornic fervour to serve the Brand and build it and sustain it, as a standard to all who shall come after thee." Immediately, Saul started speaking in slangs and praising the Voice, rejoicing that he had been counted worthy of working for the Brand. When the power of the Voice had descended on him, the Sammeritan blessed him and said, "Henceforth, you shall be called Paul Grace, for *naadom* has fallen on you and upon this foundation I will build the Brand."

The Voice was with Paul and worked mighty and great deeds through him. And the Brand grew, and many were added to their numbers. Among the deeds wrought through Paul and the servants of the Brand included a one-on-one with Junior Jesus, after his second coming and when he had visited the temple to cast lots. This feat was unprecedented, and the fame of the Brand soared and soared. The philosophers of the land saw all that Paul had done and were pleased and honoured him with a coat of many colours.

In the church at Fanoafa were many teachers and prophets: Decker who was also called Sonny, Dumor the Gbehohite, Doreenando of the House of Andoh who was one of the mighty women who had served right from the beginning of the church and Paul. As the Brand grew and grew, one day, as the servants of the Brand were meditating on the Way, the Voice spoke and said, "Set apart for me Paul Grace and Sam-Hatta the Sammenitan, for they have more work to do in unearthing and nurturing more disciplines to serve in more churches modeled after Fanoafa."

So, it came to pass that after the disciples had fasted and prayed, they sent them forth as apostles of the Voice. The two of them, sent on their way by the Voice, went down via the Appian Way and turned towards the place called *The Blood Is A Crowd,* as mentioned in the tongue of the native Ga people of the land and over the Bridge towards the Road of Liberation, proclaiming the Way of The Voice wherever they went, doing good and making disciples of all men.

The first church they planted was at the centre of The City, where Paul found and converted a young man known as Ben bar-Avle, who was full of grace and power. Ben bar-Avle was beloved of Paul.

Sometime later, Paul said to Sam-Hatta, "Let's go back and visit the brethren between Fanoafa and here and see how they are faring." Paul wanted to take Ben bar-Avle with him, but the older apostle from Sammenria wanted to keep Ben bar-Avle at The City. The two apostles had such a sharp disagreement that they parted company. Ben remained at The City but didn't lose his relationship with Paul. Paul loved Ben bar-Avle with all his heart. Paul set forth and went through Ganaria and Sankaria, eventually pitching his ministry at Labonicia, from where he continued to speak to the churches, including the church at Manasonia.

And it was at Labonica that Wofa Kapokyikyi met Paul Grace and fell in love with his sermons from the Mount every evening. Wofa wasn't alone: people from far and near would come and drink deep as the Apostle Paul taught and instructed and also brought philosophers to espouse on Plutonian and Aristocratic ideas as well as those for the downtrodden.

With the passage of time, the Brand continued to grow and expand and more were added to their numbers, including a man called Azur, from Manasonia who came wailing and sniffing and looking under the eyes of corpses. In the meantime, there arose in the land a leader of the scribes called Monney son of Frail. He was learned, both in letters worked for and those acquired.

In the eighth month of the first year of Odekuro Odieasem Nana Tutubrofo Dankwawura, Azur went looking into coffins in the house of Paul of Jos. Some of the coffins had been closed and sealed and locked in the vault. Not only did Azur open these caskets, but he did them in the open, just outside the temple gates. The harmattan winds carried the nunu scent into the corridors of the temple and permeated everywhere.

The shenanigans of Azur, with the support of the Brand, didn't go down well with the retired priests and servants of the temple. And some of the scribes, who began releasing epistles upon epistles cautioning against exorcism. Azur retorted that exorcism wasn't banned under the Torah.

Things came to a head when the major Scribe, Monney bar-Frail, released his epistle, directed towards no-one but targeted towards the discerning.

There was uproar in the land, from both Jews and Gentiles and from the Sadducees and Pharisees. Counter epistles were written and posted on the city gates and on the walls of the land. One epistle was jointly written by the Watchmen. One of the signatories was a Nyarkonite, who was a retired opener of caskets.

That is when Paul gave his seminal ecclesiastical paulogue to Azur, reminding him of the tenets of the Brand and admonishing him not to dilute the Way of the Voice, keeping it holy and sacrosanct. The Sermon covered over forty scrolls, according to the scribes whose duty it is to record the annals of the land. The Sermon chronicled the history of the church of the Brand and the canons of the Way. Paul spoke with spiritual vehemence, saying "My soul is overwhelmed with sorrow to the point of death."

And being in anguish, he spoke more earnestly, and his sweat was like drops of blood falling to the ground.

After the Sermon, there was uproar in the land, with the Watchmen saying perhaps the apostle had been affected by his association with the house of Jos. And when the Nyarkonite, who was used as an example of how not to behave in the Way, came to affirm the methods of Azur the Manasonian, the people of the land looked up to the heavens, for a word from the Voice.

In the meantime, the people reached out for their favourite book in such moments: the book of Nahum. Even Wofa Kapokyikyi, who is not usually bereft of words, is reading Nahum.

Hmmm…

As for Monney bar-Frail, he won't be forgetting his epistle in a hurry, as we await the casting of lots soon. Will it be the one epistle that determines how he gets to manage the letters after his name, either procured or awarded?

Till I come your way another day with another sebitical, I remain:

Sebitically yours,

Kapokyikyiwofaase

WHAT WOFA EYE SEE SAW IN SOWETO

A few months after Odekuro Odieasem Nana Tutubrofo Dankwawura ascended the throne of Sikaman, and during one particularly cool evening as he sat under the royal palms in the gardens of the Ahenfie that sits atop the hill beside the Ehyire river, as he sipped his sobolo fortified with a little something for his stomach, he reflected on the hard and long journey from his days when he was called Willie. He remembered names, names, some of which had been consigned to the pages of time. He thought of the son of He Who Had No Father, his bosom friend. He sighed.

His mental eyes went over the land. His heart was heavy, but his soul was grateful. Grateful that there still remained time and chance to appreciate the loyal ones who stood with him. His mind saw and he said to himself, *I see.*

But Odekuro could not rest, his mind was restless. His beloved Gholoriah saw her husband in deep thoughts and knew she had to leave him to battle on, trusting as always that when he needed her, he would pour forth his inner thoughts and share with her.

Later that night, Odekuro tossed in bed. He could not sleep. Then he woke up and ordered that the book of the chronicles be brought in, the book that contained the records of his struggles right from the days when he tangoed with The Giants, both Gentle and Humble. He wanted to know if there was anyone in there whose dedication and loyalty had not been rewarded.

And, lo, there in the annals were found that in the land of Osei, there was a man who had provided fuel for the soldiers of the struggle, who had given to the troops, who had defended the flag and colours of the elephant that Odekuro rode to victory.

"What honour and recognition was given to this man, whom you call Wofa Eye See?"

"Nothing has been done for him," his attendants answered.

"What?!" Odekuro bellowed.

He called for his chief adviser, also known as The Wind, *m frama.*

"What can we do for Wofa Eye See that would be commensurate with his valour and dedication?"

The Wind responded, "Long may you live, oh Odekuro! You have asked right. For just yesterday, one of your advisers told me that Wofa Eye See loves to dance and also to travel."

"Ah!" the King beamed, "then we shall dispatch him to the land south of the Limpopo, to dance with Jay Zee the Zumite, who resides in Soweto."

So, it came to pass that to Soweto went Wofa Eye See.

As for all that Wofa Eye See saw in Soweto, all that he did and the Sikamanians that he catered in the land south of the Limpopo, are they not written in the book of the annals of the emissaries to the Zumite?

However, Wofa Eye See saw that the people of Sikaman do not read and, being afraid that they might not read the annals, he decided to tell his own stories of what had been recorded about him in the annals and what he saw in Soweto.

So, it came to pass that when Wofa Eye See returned to Sikaman on his annual visit to the Temple, there was much drumming and dancing and jubilation that he had wrought exploits in the land south of Limpopo. And Wofa Eye See, wearing a linen batakari, danced before the Lord and his people with all his might, and the shout of rejoicing went up from the empeepeetude that thronged the courtyard of the assembly, with the catchphrase "Wofa Eye See! Wofa Eye See!"

The louder the chorus, the harder Wofa Eye See danced, dancing just as the Zumite did. And all who saw remarked in admiration, saying to one another "Indeed! Wofa Eye See has been with Jay Zee!"

Then a voice arose among the empeepeetude, saying "Wofa Eye See, speak to us, before we die!" The chorus was picked up and soon there was a loud, repetition of "Wofa Eye See, speak to us, before we die!" reverberating across the courtyard.

Wofa Eye See, with sweat on his brows and same dripping down his beard and running down on the collar of his robes, looked upon the empeepeetude and smiled his blessings, saying to himself, Oh see how they love me!

Then he went to the nearby Sono Mountain and sat then. The empeepeetude still followed him and gathered around him. Then he began to teach them, saying:

"Blessed are the holder of empeeple cards, for their time in come.

"Blessed are those who have mourned in the past under the Hedzolites for they will now be comforted.

"Blessed are the foot-soldiers, for they shall be catered for first.

"Blessed are the owners of the new patriotic passports, for they are more Sikamanian than others.

"Blessed are those who hunger and thirst for political jobs, for their mouths shall be filled with sobolo, asaana and a little pito.

"For man shall not live by bread alone, but with a little Blue band and jam.

"Blessed are the Patrionians, for theirs is the kingdom of God.

"Blessed are you when people truly say that you used to speak against the favouritism that you desire now. Rejoice and be glad, for your time to chop has come and great is your reward here in Sikaman and in the land south of the Limpopo. For in the same way, they lamented and whined against the Hedzolites whose song Yentie Obia they rejected. Know ye, and be comforted, that Sikamanians have the memory of ants, and forget as quickly as the morning dew lasts.

"Do not think that I have come to abolish the ways of politics in Sikaman. I have not come to abolish them but to fulfil them and entrenched them. Verily, verily, I say onto you, until Nii Ayi Bonte relinquishes his stool, not the least of you shall be overlooked for a job before another without an empeepee card. For you are more Sikamanian than all. Take it or leave it."

The empeepeetude heard these words and were glad. And they went their way, rejoicing and singing the praises of Wofa Eye See.

But some wondered if Wofa Eye See said the mind of Odekuro Tutubrofo. As to that question in their minds, I will leave you to reflect on same, till I come your way with another sebitical.

I still remain:

Sebitically yours,

Kapokyikyiwofaase